MALTA *on board* the U.S.S. CONSTITUTION. Comm. J.D.ELLICT. 1837   J.G.Evans

GEORGE WASHINGTON

AMERICAN ICON

ICON SERIES

THE CAREER OF GEORGE WASHINGTON WAS ONE OF EXTRAORDINARY drama and moral consequence. He lived in the vortex of history as an active participant in the birth of a nation and the forging of a modern form of democratic government. His role in America's War for Independence and his leadership of the new republic earned him heroic status within his own lifetime.

Two centuries later, the gulf between his Revolutionary era and our own seems vast, even unfathomable. His nobility and steely fortitude suggest a hero in the classical mode rather than a modern warrior-statesman. Here is the enigma of George Washington, and the wellspring of his enduring fame: in a time of crisis and decision he comported himself like a messenger from another, distant age of heroes.

By birth and upbringing, George Washington was part of Virginia's rural gentry, an elite that modeled its way of life on England's provincial aristocracy. He was born on his father's plantation at Popes Creek, in Westmoreland County, Virginia, on February 22, 1732. The Washington family was descended from two brothers, John and Lawrence, who came from Northamptonshire, England, in 1657. George's father, Augustine Washington, a prosperous planter and entrepreneur, was married twice. His first marriage, with Jane Butler in 1715, produced four children, two of whom, Lawrence and Augustine, grew to manhood. His second marriage, with Mary Ball in 1730, produced six children—George (the eldest), Betty, Samuel, John, Charles, and Mildred, who died in infancy.

From 1735 to 1739, George lived at the estate that is now called Mount Vernon, on the Potomac River, and afterwards at the estate on the Rappahannock, nearly opposite Fredericksburg, Virginia. His father died at age 49 on April 12, 1743, leaving the estate on the Potomac to Lawrence; the eleven-year-old George inherited the much smaller estate on the Rappahannock. George was raised thereafter by his mother, who instilled in him the virtues of justice, self-discipline, conscientiousness, and prompt decision.

Opposite: **George Washington in the Uniform of a British Colonial Colonel** *(1772) by* **Charles Willson Peale.** *This iconic image of Washington at age 40 is the only likeness known to have been rendered before the outbreak of the Revolutionary War. Painted nearly fourteen years after Washington had resigned his position as colonel in the Virginia Regiment, the portrait places Washington at his earliest battleground in the Ohio River valley.*

Below: **Early Washington family coat of arms from the parish church of Warton in Lancashire.**

Above: In 1748, while surveying the Fairfax holdings in the Allegheny Mountains, Washington wrote in his diary, "We were agreeably surpris'd at the sight of thirty odd Indians coming from War with only one Scalp. We had some Liquor with us of which we gave them Part it elevating there Spirits put them in the Humour of Dauncing of whom we had a War Daunce." Below: Fishing hooks and line belonging to George Washington.

George's legal guardian and mentor was his half-brother Lawrence. Lawrence was educated in England, and he married the daughter of Colonel William Fairfax, who owned the neighboring plantation of Belvoir, and became agent for the extensive Fairfax lands in the colony. Lawrence served with Fairfax in the Royal Navy, where he also made the acquaintance of Admiral Edward Vernon, after whom Mount Vernon was named.

Washington spent his youth on the plantation, busying himself with hunting, fishing, and a little reading. Due to the family's straitened circumstances after his father's death, he did not go to school in England like Lawrence or even attend the nearby College of William and Mary. His Virginia schoolmasters gave him a solid, practical education, and George excelled in math and law. He was meticulous in the preparation of his schoolbooks, and by his teens he had mastered the basic principles of surveying, a science which demands accuracy and detail.

At the age of sixteen, he set out on a surveying expedition across the Blue Ridge Mountains to the Shenandoah Valley of northern Virginia with Colonel William Fairfax. That same year, Washington was named surveyor of the Fairfax property, and an appointment as public surveyor of Culpeper County, Virginia, followed in July of the next year. He spent much of the next three years on the colony's western frontier and developed an early appreciation of the value of this fertile region. By age eighteen he had claimed 1,450 acres of his own in the lower Shenandoah Valley.

Above: General Braddock's bloodstained sash, which he presented to Washington as he lay dying.

In 1751, he traveled to Barbados with Lawrence, who was gravely ill, probably with tuberculosis, and stayed until January 1752; while there, George survived an attack of smallpox which left him marked for life but also immune to that scourge of armies. Lawrence died the following year, having named George his executor. George initially signed a lease with Lawrence's widow, Ann Fairfax Washington Lee, to rent Mount Vernon for 15,000 pounds of tobacco or cash equivalent per year; the estate became his upon her death in 1761.

In October 1753, amid disputes between France and England over the boundaries of their American possessions, Washington was sent by Lieutenant Governor Robert Dinwiddie of Virginia on a perilous mission to warn the French away from their new posts

along the Ohio River in western Pennsylvania. He returned to Williamsburg in January to submit his report to Dinwiddie. He was appointed lieutenant-colonel of a Virginia regiment in March 1754 and led a mission to Fort Duquesne. The shots fired during a skirmish in May marked the opening volleys of the Seven Years' (French and Indian) War, which was officially declared in 1756. On July 3, 1754, Washington's troops suffered a major defeat at the hands of the French and Indians in the Battle of Great Meadows, and he was forced to surrender at Fort Necessity.

The British general Edward Braddock arrived in Virginia in February 1755, and Washington soon became a member of his staff, first as colonel and three months later as volunteer aide-de-camp. In the calamitous defeat of July 1755 at the

Below: Detail from **Washington as a Captain in the French and Indian War** *(1849–56) by **Junius Brutus Stearns**. Though painted a century later, this rendering of the unexpected defeat of Braddock's forces on July 9, 1755, captures the drama of this critical episode in Washington's military career. As the mortally wounded Braddock collapses into the arms of his comrades, Washington (seated on horseback) leads the men on to battle for their lives.*

Above: Painting of Mount Vernon (c. 1792), attributed to Edward Savage. This is one of the few depictions of the estate's bucolic splendor painted while Washington was still alive. The slave quarters is the brown building to the right. Opposite: Washington's natural talents as a surveyor are reflected in his balanced designs for the mansion and surrounding gardens of Mount Vernon. His surveying instruments are shown here with Samuel Vaughan's 1787 journal and plan.

Monongahela River, in which Braddock perished, Washington fought with the fiery energy which normally lay hidden beneath his calm and unruffled exterior, and was credited with saving the expedition from annihilation. On August 14, he was appointed Colonel and Commander of the Virginia regiment, charged with the task of defending "a frontier of more than 350 miles, with 700 men." The French abandoned Fort Duquesne on November 23, 1758, burning it as they left, and Washington led an advance guard of two Virginia regiments who occupied and rebuilt the stronghold, which was renamed Fort Pitt (now Pittsburgh). He resigned his commission in November, fully initiated in the techniques—and frustrations—of frontier warfare.

On January 6, 1759, he married Martha (Dandridge) Custis, a widow with two children, John Parke Custis, aged four, and Martha Parke Custis, aged two.

Left: Miniature portraits of Washington's two stepchildren, Martha Parke Custis (left) and John Parke Custis (right).

The BLOODY MASSACRE perpetrated in King—t—Street BOSTON on March 5th 1770 by a party of the 29th REG.

BUTCHER'S HALL

Engrav'd Printed & Sold by PAUL REVERE BOSTON

Unhappy BOSTON! see thy Sons deplore,
Thy hallow'd Walks besmear'd with guiltless Gore:
While faithless P——n and his savage Bands,
With murd'rous Rancour stretch their bloody Hands;
Like fierce Barbarians grinning o'er their Prey,
Approve the Carnage and enjoy the Day.

If scalding drops from Rage from Anguish Wrung
If speechless Sorrows lab'ring for a Tongue,
Or if a weeping World can ought appease
The plaintive Ghosts of Victims such as these;
The Patriot's copious Tears for each are shed,
A glorious Tribute which embalms the Dead.

But know FATE summons to that awful Goal,
Where JUSTICE strips the Murd'rer of his Soul:
Should venal C——ts the scandal of the Land,
Snatch the relentless Villain from her Hand,
Keen Execrations on this Plate inscrib'd,
Shall reach a JUDGE who never can be brib'd.

The unhappy Sufferers were Mess. SAML GRAY SAML MAVERICK, JAMS CALDWELL, CRISPUS ATTUCKS & PATK CARR
Killed. Six wounded; two of them (CHRISTR MONK & JOHN CLARK) Mortally

Washington's Rules of Civility

As first citizen in both government and society, George Washington exhibited exemplary social graces. He had learned these as early as age 13, when he copied down the 110 maxims of "The Rules of Civility and Decent Behavior in Company and Conversation." Culled from a 1595 Jesuit text later translated into English, these precepts guided his education as a gentleman, soldier, and statesman. Here are some excerpts:

- Every Action done in Company ought to be with Some Sign of Respect, to those that are Present.

- Sleep not when others Speak, Sit not when others stand, Speak not when you should hold your Peace, walk not when others Stop.

- Shew not yourself glad at the Misfortune of another though he were your enemy.

- In Speaking to men of Quality do not lean nor Look them full in the Face, nor approach too near them at least Keep a full Pace from them.

- Use no Reproachful Language against any one neither Curse nor Revile.

- Put not another bit into your Mouth till the former be Swallowed let not your Morsels be too big for your jowls.

- Labour to keep alive in your Breast that Little Spark of Celestial fire called Conscience.

*Opposite: **The Bloody Massacre perpetrated in Boston on March 5th 1770**, printed by **Paul Revere. Famous as the Boston silversmith who embarked on the "midnight ride" to warn of the approach of British troops, Revere was a leading anti-British propagandist in the years leading up to the outbreak of the American Revolution. Five townspeople were killed in the Boston Massacre, an event which galvanized colonial resistance to British rule.***

Martha brought considerable wealth to Washington's already prosperous plantations at Mount Vernon, which they proceeded to develop and enlarge. A member and vestryman of the Established (Episcopal) Church, a slave-holder, a strict but considerate master, and a widely trusted man of affairs, Washington embodied the eighteenth-century ideal of the genteel Virginia planter. He was an avid foxhunter and went out with his hounds as often as several times a week, especially during winter months when there was less activity on the farm.

England owed a huge debt at the end of the Seven Years' War, and for King George III the most expedient way to repay it was by imposing onerous taxes on his American subjects. At this crucial time for the American colonies, Washington was elected Fairfax County's representative to Virginia's House of Burgesses, an assembly that met in Williamsburg. Washington was present in the House of Burgesses on May 29, 1765, when Patrick Henry introduced his famous resolutions against the Stamp Act. England's increasingly heavy-handed measures to enforce its policy of tax and rule would soon spark open rebellion in such incidents as the Boston Massacre of 1770 and the Boston Tea Party of December 1773.

Above: Colonial currency printed by Benjamin Franklin.

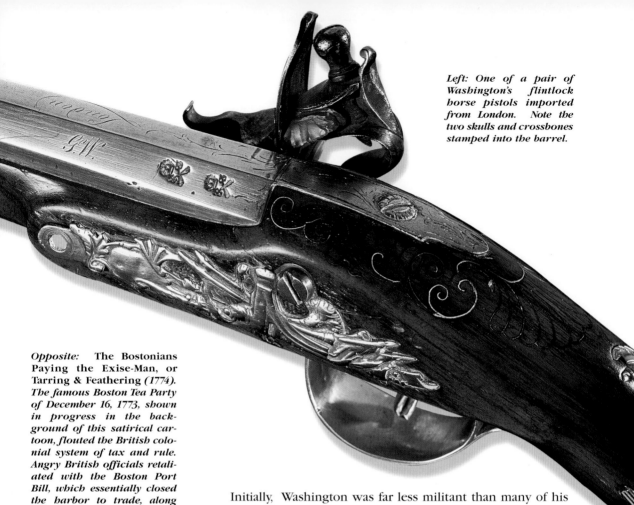

Left: One of a pair of Washington's flintlock horse pistols imported from London. Note the two skulls and crossbones stamped into the barrel.

Opposite: **The Bostonians Paying the Exise-Man, or Tarring & Feathering** *(1774). The famous Boston Tea Party of December 16, 1773, shown in progress in the background of this satirical cartoon, flouted the British colonial system of tax and rule. Angry British officials retaliated with the Boston Port Bill, which essentially closed the harbor to trade, along with other harsh measures that pushed Massachusetts into open rebellion.*

Below: General Washington applied copper nameplates to trunks he purchased for use as military chests soon after assuming command of the Continental Army.

Initially, Washington was far less militant than many of his fellow colonists. He recognized that British intransigence on the issue of taxation could lead to war—"more blood will be spilled on this occasion if the ministry are determined to push matters to extremity, than history has ever yet furnished instances of in the annals of North America"—but refrained from declaring in favor of independence until the course of events made the adoption of any other course impossible.

He attended the Virginia Provincial Convention at Williamsburg in August 1774 and was appointed one of seven delegates to the First Continental Congress at Philadelphia. In May 1775, he attended the Second Continental Congress, where he served on committees for fortifying New York, collecting badly needed ammunition, raising money, and formulating army regulations. In June, after the fighting at Lexington and Concord, the Congress resolved that the colonies ought to be put in a position of defense, and the first practical step was to select a commander-in-chief of the Continental Army.

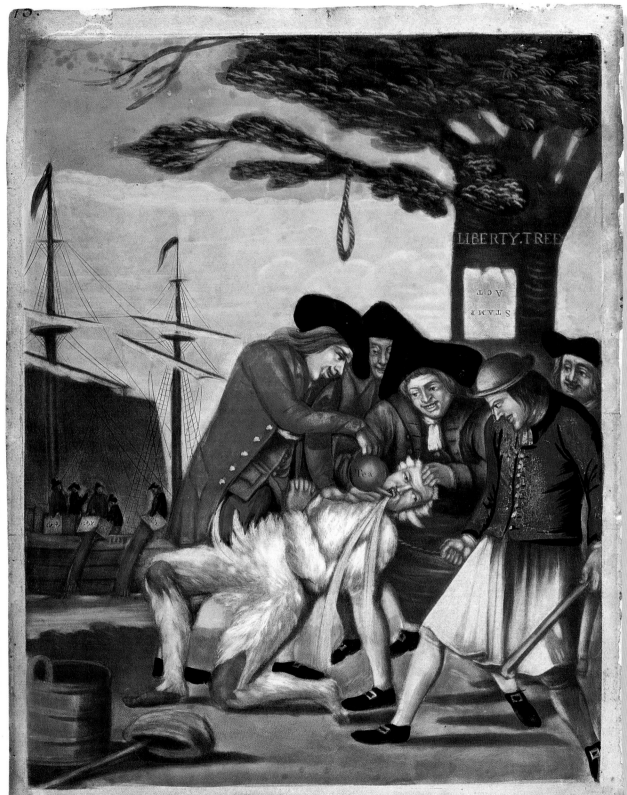

The BOSTONIAN'S Paying the EXCISE-MAN, or TARRING & FEATHERING

Plate I.

London, Printed for Rob.t Sayer & J.Bennett, Map & Printseller, N.o 53, Fleet Street, as the Act directs 31.Oct.r 1774.

Washington was the unanimous choice; he had a rare combination of distinguished political and military experience (and at six feet three inches, he cut a dashing figure in his dress uniform and sword). He accepted the position but refused any salary, asking only for reimbursement of his expenses. He was commissioned on June 17, 1775, the day of the Battle of Bunker Hill, a signal event in the escalation of the war. By the time he took command of the Continental Army at Cambridge, Massachusetts, on July 3—the twenty-first anniversary of his surrender to the French at Fort Necessity—troops had gathered from far and wide to fight against the British garrison in Boston.

Washington planned the expeditions against Canada under Richard Montgomery and Benedict Arnold, and sent out privateers to harass British commerce. His troops drove the British out of Boston and occupied the city in March 1776, after an eight-month siege. He had matured into a general and statesman of the first order, and from then on he was regarded as the most influential man of the continent.

Passage of the Declaration of Independence was announced on July 4, 1776, with the ringing of a bell that had been imported from London twenty-three years earlier by the Provincial Assembly of Philadelphia. It bore a biblical inscription freighted with contemporary significance: "Proclaim liberty throughout the land, unto all the inhabitants thereof." The Declaration put to rest any lingering hopes of reconciliation with the British and

Opposite: In September of 1776, within days of the British capture of Manhattan Island, a fire began in a tavern down by the docks and, driven by the wind, soon swept northward. By dawn, fully a quarter of the city's buildings had been consumed. British authorities blamed the fire on revolutionary arsonists and rounded up about 200 suspects, including Nathan Hale, who was shortly hanged as a spy. The island remained in British hands until the end of 1783.

Below: Washington Crossing the Delaware (1853). Based on a life-size mural painted by the German artist Emanuel Leutze in 1849, this engraving is a dramatic recreation of one of the critical events of the Revolutionary War. Its fanciful, even romantic elements caused a sensation in America, and the image has been copied relentlessly.

inspired America to fight on with new determination and unity. Washington had the document read aloud to each of his brigades on July 9; that evening, a lead statue of King George III in New York City was toppled by a mob who promised to melt it down for bullets "to be used in the cause of independence."

For the rebels, however, the prospect of war against Europe's mightiest empire was terrifying: Could 19,000 determined but untrained and ill-armed recruits take on an army of 32,000 seasoned British soldiers? In August of 1776, the bulk of the British force landed on Staten Island in preparation for General William Howe's assault upon New York. On August 27, Howe outflanked and defeated Washington's troops in Brooklyn, killing some 2,000 Americans. Taking advantage of a momentary lull in Howe's campaign, Washington quietly evacuated the remainder of his troops to Manhattan, slipping across the East River under the cover of a heavy fog on the night of August 29. As New York fell to the advancing British in the succeeding days, Washington was forced to continue his retreat, so he led his demoralized and dwindling forces up the Hudson River, then back south through New Jersey and across the Delaware River into Pennsylvania. Howe and his army were never far behind, but Washington succeeded in denying his enemy the opportunity of a decisive engagement. It was a cat-and-mouse game, and Howe would have to pounce in order to win.

Above: **Washington and his Generals at Yorktown (1781–1783) by Charles Willson Peale (detail). Lord Cornwallis selected Yorktown as a base for its deep-water frontage along the York River and strategic proximity to the Chesapeake Bay. But Washington brilliantly anticipated that Yorktown was vulnerable to siege and blockade if he could muster sufficient land and naval forces. This painting, made shortly after the decisive events of 1781, is based on Peale's first-hand observations of the site. Opposite: Miniature portraits of George and Martha Washington, one of Washington's spurs, and the key to the Bastille. The last, the actual iron key to the infamous Paris political prison, was presented to Washington by his great friend and political ally, the Marquis de Lafayette. Inspired by the American Revolution, in 1789 a Parisian mob stormed the Bastille and freed its hundreds of prisoners. The following year, the Marquis de Lafayette ordered the prison demolished and sent Washington the key, now a priceless historical relic, as a token of his appreciation. The Bastille key still hangs at Mount Vernon today.**

Even in retreat, Washington displayed remarkable skill, even greatness, as a military strategist and leader. He knew from his experience in the French and Indian War that if he could save his army from annihilation in open battle, they had a chance of eventual triumph. In the meantime, he relied on small victories to keep up the spirits of his troops and confound the enemy. On Christmas night of 1776, he boldly re-crossed the Delaware River and surprised a garrison of Hessian mercenaries in Trenton the next morning, capturing 918 and killing 30. Remarkably, only five of his own men were wounded and none died in the fighting. He struck his pursuers again at Princeton on January 3, 1777, and afterward set up winter quarters at Morristown so as to block the advance of British forces toward Philadelphia. He handled his army with vigor in the defeats at the Brandywine and Germantown in the fall of 1777 and tenaciously held his strategic position at Valley Forge through the punishing winter of 1777–1778, despite the misery of his men and the impotence of a Congress that had by this time abandoned Philadelphia.

A worsening pessimism that culminated in the treason of Benedict Arnold was a serious addition to Washington's burdens, for it was clear that others were on the verge of abandoning the American cause. Washington's close friendship with the French marquis de Lafayette inspired jealousy among his officers, as did the deference he showed toward the other foreign officers upon whom the success of the war depended. When a plot to replace Washington with General Horatio Gates as commander-in-chief came to light, a disgruntled Irish volunteer named Thomas Conway was left to shoulder both the responsibility and the disgrace. The intrigue known as Conway's Cabal actually wound up strengthening Washington's position as commander-in-chief by showcasing his dignified conduct even in the face of anonymous slander.

Left: Uniform worn by General George Washington. This is believed to be the uniform he wore when he resigned his commission at Annapolis in 1783.

The 1778 treaty of alliance with France came at a critical moment and marked a turning point in the war. Indeed, the nation against which Washington had battled in his youth would soon prove indispensable to America's final victory, and Washington embraced these new circumstances with alacrity. The British evacuation of Philadelphia in June 1778 was spurred on by Washington's capable handling of his troops in the engagement at Monmouth, New Jersey. The end of the war was finally in sight.

Washington had been the mainspring of the war from the beginning, and had borne far more than his share of its burdens and discouragements. Fittingly, he could claim full credit for the siege and battle of Yorktown, Virginia, which resulted in the surrender of Cornwallis on October 19, 1781. Although a formal peace was not signed until September 1783, there was no more significant fighting after Yorktown.

Victory was at hand, but many soldiers in the Continental Army had grown dissatisfied with their treatment over the course of the war. Unpaid, under-equipped, and exhausted after years of danger and grinding routine, they had endured the worst that war can give—and Washington's continual appeals to the Congress had gone unanswered all too often. The officers wanted back pay and pensions. In the spring of 1782, a movement arose to march westward and appropriate vacant public lands as part compensation for arrears of pay, and even hail Washington as

Washington as an Entrepreneur

In addition to his other achievements, George Washington was a major plantation owner, one of the largest property owners in Virginia, and passionately interested in new developments in agriculture. When he was not fulfilling his duties as soldier or statesman, he spent every moment he could at Mount Vernon overseeing the estate. He built a distillery, harvested millions of pounds of herring and shad from nearby rivers, and experimented with about 60 different crops, developing a seven-year crop rotation system that insured the revitalization of the soil. He also has been credited with introducing the mule to the United States. At the end of his life, he wrote of his hope that "the manly employment of agriculture" would replace "the waste of war and the rage of conquest."

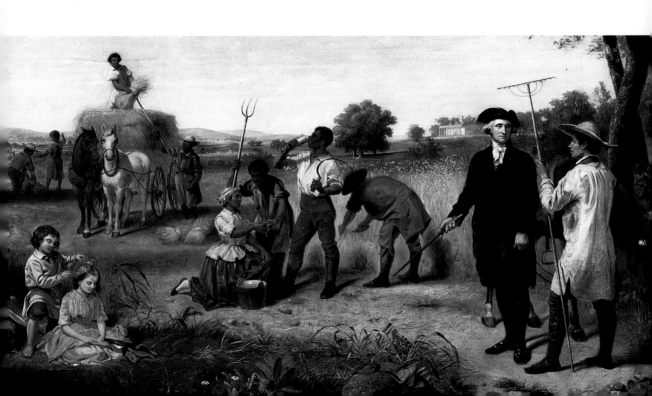

Bust of George Washington (1785) by Jean-Antoine Houdon. The foremost sculptor of the French Enlightenment, Houdon was sent from Paris by Thomas Jefferson and Benjamin Franklin at the behest of the governor of Virginia to create the life-size marble statue of Washington which now graces the Virginia Capitol. After obtaining the plaster life mask needed to create the final sculpture, Houdon presented the original terra-cotta bust to his subject as a parting gift. Martha Washington's granddaughter Nelly Custis later recalled: "I was only six years old at that time. . . . I was passing the white servants Hall and saw as I thought the Corpse of one I considered my Father; I went in, and found the General extended on his back on a large table, a sheet over him, except his face, on which Houdon was engaged in putting on plaster to form the cast. Quills were in the nostrils. I was very much alarmed until I was told that it was a bust, a likeness of the General, and would not injure him."

their king. When Washington got word of their intentions, he put an immediate end to the whole affair with his withering Newburgh Addresses, in which he admonished his supporters, "if you have any regard for yourself or posterity, or respect for me, to banish these thoughts from your mind, and never communicate, as from yourself or anyone else, a sentiment of the like nature."

On June 8, 1783, Washington addressed a letter to the governors, pointing out changes in the existing form of government which he believed to be necessary, and urging "an indissoluble union of the states under one federal head," the adoption of a suitable peacetime military establishment, and a national commitment to "those mutual concessions which are requisite to the general prosperity."

An organization of former army officers elected Washington as the first president-general of their newly formed Society of the Cincinnati, in 1783. He accepted the honorary position but was later embarrassed by the Society's hereditary membership restrictions, which critics such as Washington's friend Thomas Jefferson derided as contrary to the nation's new, egalitarian spirit. The Society, which takes its name from the famous Roman soldier-turned-farmer, still claims about 3,500 members, each of whom is the eldest son of a direct descendant of a Revolutionary War officer.

Washington bade a formal farewell to his army on November 2, and a month later gathered with officers. In a second-floor room just above Fraunces Tavern in Lower Manhattan, the general told his troops, "With a heart full of love and gratitude, I now take leave of you." He resigned his commission on December 23, 1783, voluntarily surrendering his sword to the Congress in Annapolis, Maryland, and vowing never to take "any share in public business hereafter." He retired to Mount Vernon eager to resume the simple pleasures of domestic life and attend to his plantation after an eight-year absence.

Even in retirement, however, Washington led an active life. The following December, he attended a conference on Potomac River navigation at Annapolis. He was presented a

The Image of a Leader

George Washington was a man of commanding presence—unusually tall for his era, strappingly handsome, and of noble posture and bearing. Here is Lord William Fairfax's description of the young Washington:

[He stands as] straight as an Indian, measuring 6 foot 2 inches in his stockings, and weighing 175 pounds. . . . His frame is padded with well developed muscles, indicating great strength. His bones and joints are large as are his hands and feet. He is wide shouldered. . . . His head is well shaped, though not large, but is gracefully poised on a superb neck. A large and straight and rather prominent nose; blue-gray penetrating eyes which are widely separated and overhung by a heavy brow. A pleasing and benevolent though commanding countenance. . . . In conversation he looks you full in the face, is deliberate, deferential, and engaging. His demeanor at all times composed and dignified. His movements and gestures are graceful, his walk majestic, and he is a splendid horseman.

Inset, top: Gold watch used by Washington during his presidency.

Below: Washington's brass telescope, possibly the one he used at the Battle of Princeton.

George Washington Bids Farewell to His Officers at Fraunces Tavern

On entering the room and finding himself surrounded by his old companions in arms, who had shared with him so many scenes of hardship, difficulty, and danger, his agitated feelings overcame his usual self-command. Filling a glass of wine and turning upon them his benignant but saddened countenance, "With a heart full of love and gratitude," said he, "I now take leave of you, most devoutly wishing that your latter days may be as prosperous and happy as your former ones have been glorious and honorable."

Having drunk this farewell benediction, he added with emotion, "I cannot come to each of you to take my leave, but shall be obliged if each of you will come and take me by the hand." General Knox, who was nearest, was the first to advance. Washington, affected even to tears, grasped his hand and gave him a brother's embrace.

In the same affectionate manner he took leave severally of the rest. Not a word was spoken. The deep feeling and manly tenderness of these veterans in the parting moment could find no utterance in words.

(From Washington Irving's
Life of Washington)

gift of stock from the James River and Potomac River canal companies, and he agonized over whether it was proper to accept it. Eventually he resolved to donate the stock to the college that later became known as Washington and Lee University. He was later elected president of the Potomac Company.

On March 23–25, 1785, he hosted the Mount Vernon Conference, which resulted in a compact between Maryland and Virginia regulating commerce on Chesapeake Bay and the Potomac River. The new nation lacked an effective national government, so any commerce between states needed lengthy negotiation, almost as if they were separate countries. Washington responded by publicly advocating a strong national government.

In May 1787, he attended the Federal Convention at

Philadelphia as a Virginia delegate—abandoning, in his friend James Madison's words, "the honorable retreat to which he had retired, and [risking] the reputation he had so deserved." Washington was at once elected the assembly's presiding officer by a unanimous vote. Though he took little part in the debate, his presence and support were critical in the creation and ratification of the Constitution. "Be assured," James Monroe told Thomas Jefferson, "his influence carried this government." On June 21, 1788, New Hampshire became the ninth and deciding state to ratify the Constitution (Virginia followed suit on June 25).

Once the framework of the new government had been determined and the time came to choose the first President of the United States, there was no hesitation: Washington was elected by unanimous vote of the Electoral College. He was officially notified of the election results at Mount Vernon on April 14, 1789, and was inaugurated at Federal Hall in New York City on April 30, with John Adams of Massachusetts as his vice-president. Washington surrounded himself with a distinguished cabinet (this use of the word came into currency during his administration) including Secretary of State Thomas Jefferson, Alexander Hamilton at Treasury, John Jay as chief justice, and Secretary of War Henry Knox.

On August 25, 1789, Washington's mother, Mary Ball Washington, died at Fredericksburg, Virginia. Though their relationship had been strained in her final years, and she had frequently complained that he had neglected his duties toward her, he loved her dearly and was deeply shaken by her loss.

Below: This miniature features a "GW" cipher over a lock of reddish hair said to be that of George Washington.

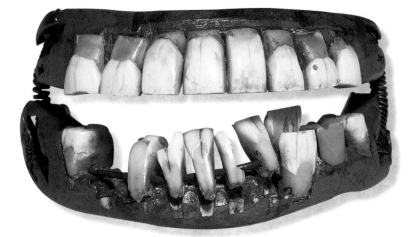

Left: Washington was plagued with dental problems for most of his life. During his last decade, he wore this set of dentures, which are made of human teeth and carved cow teeth and elephant ivory. Mounted on a lead base, they were awkward to wear and apparently a major embarrassment for the president.

Above: **The Washington Family** *(c. 1789–98), attributed to Edward Savage. This painting depicts Washington's final retirement at Mount Vernon, surrounded by Martha and her two grandchildren, Nelly and George Washington Custis. Washington's personal servant Christopher Sheels is shown in the background at far right. On the table unfolds the plan of Federal City, later Washington D.C., drawn by the French architect L'Enfant. Washington worked closely with him on the design of the city and also set the cornerstone of the Capitol.*

Despite his fervent wish to return to the domestic tranquillity of Mount Vernon, Washington was persuaded by his friends and advisors to stay on for a second term, and in December 1792, he was unanimously re-elected. In September 1790, Washington moved from New York to Philadelphia, the nation's new (temporary) capital. On September 18, 1793, he laid the cornerstone of the Capitol Building in Federal City, which in 1800 became the seat of government and was renamed Washington, District of Columbia.

Throughout his two terms as president, Washington remained committed to the task of building a strong central government. He faced his greatest challenge in 1794, when grain farmers in western Pennsylvania rose up against recently imposed federal excise taxes on whiskey. Washington responded by ordering the insurgents to disperse and requesting the

The elegant large dining room at Mount Vernon was used for formal dinners. Washington half jokingly complained that his home was a "well resorted tavern," and that due to the stream of visitors, he and Martha had not dined alone for twenty years.

Negros

Belonging to George Washington in his own right and by Marriage

G.W			Dower		
Names	ages	Remarks	Names	ages	Remarks
Tradesmen &c			**Tradesmen &c**		
Nat . Smith		His wife Lucy . D.R. dor	Tom Davis B. lay.r		wife at Mr Lear
George .. Do		Ditto .. Lydia R.T. Do	Simms .. Carp.		Do . Daphne . Fren
Isaac. Carp.		.... Kitty Dairy dt	Cyrus ... Post.r		Do . Lucy . R.T. ...
James .. Do	40	..... Darcus M.H. GW	Wilson .. Ditto	15	no wife
Sambo Do		...... Agnes R.T. dor	Godfray. Cart.r		wife . Mima . Mr H.
Davy .. Do		..... Edy . U.T. GW	James .. Do		Do ... Alla . Do
Joe .. Do		..... Dolshy Spin dor	Hanson . Dist.r		No wife ..
Tom .. Coop.r		..... Nanny M.H. GW	Peter .. Do		. Ditto
Moses . Do		No Wife	Nat .. Do		Ditto
Jacob ... Do		. Ditto	Daniel . Do		Ditto
George. Gard.r		His wife Sall . D.R. dor	Timothy . Do		
Harry . Do		No wife	Ha. Joe . Ditch.r		Wife Sylla D.R ..
Boatswain Ditto		His wife Mortilla Spin GW	Chrys ... H. Ser		Do .. May Wests
Dundee . Do		His wife at Mr Lears	Marcus . Do		no Wife
Charles . Do		. Ditto ... Fanny U.F. dor	Lucy . Cook		Husbd H. Frank ..
Ben .. Do		. Ditto .. Penny R.T. GW	Nelly .. Charlotte . Serv.t		No Husband
Ben .. Miller		Ditto .. Sinah Mr H dor	Sall ... H.r M		No husband Do
Forrester Do		No Wife	Caroline . Do		Husbd . Peter Hardm
Nathan Cook	31	Wife .. Peg . M.H. GW	Nelly .. Mill.r		Do . Isaac Carp.r
Wm Muclus B. lay.r		Do .. Captn Marshalls	Alce .. Spin.r		Charles . Freeman
Juba . Carter		No wife	Betty Davis . Do		Mrs Washington's . Do
Matilda Spinner		Boson . Ditcher	Dolshy		Husbd Joe . Carp.r
Frank H. Serv.		Wife . Lucy . Cook	Anna		Do . Lis at George
Will ... Shoem.r		Lama . no wife	Judy ..	21	No Husband
			Delphy		Ditto . Do
			Peter . Cam Knit.r		No wife
			Alla .. Do		Husbd James Cart.r
Amount	**24**		**Amount**	**28**	
Mansion House			**Mansion House**		
Payed Labour			Will		Wife aggy D.R.
Frank ...	80	No Wife	Joe . Postil.r		Do . Sall . R.T.
Gunner ...	90	Wife . Judy . R.T. GW	Mike ..		No wife . son to L
Sam . Cook	40	Ditto . Alce M.H. Do	Sinah ..		Husbd Miller Ben
			Mima ..		Do . Godfrey Mag
			Lucy ..		No Husband
			Grace ..		Husbd M. Lears .
			Letty ..		No husband

governors of Pennsylvania, Maryland, New Jersey, and Virginia to mobilize militias to quell the so-called Whiskey Rebellion. He also commanded several thousand troops as they marched into Pennsylvania, becoming the first and only sitting president to lead an army in the field of battle. Though the actual use of force was never required to diffuse the rebellion, Washington clearly established the federal government's right to enforce its laws.

In 1796, a weary President Washington decided not to run for re-election. Once again voluntarily relinquishing power (as he had done when resigning his commission as commander-in-chief of the army in 1783), he set such a compelling example that no subsequent president sought a third term until Franklin Delano Roosevelt did so in 1940, amidst the outbreak of World War II. (The 22nd Amendment to the U.S. Constitution, establishing a two-term limit for the presidency, was signed into law in 1951.) Shortly after making this decision, Washington asked Alexander Hamilton to redraft a valedictory speech that he had originally intended to give at the end of his first term. First published in September 1796 and reprinted innumerable times since, Washington's Farewell Address stressed the need for a strong central government and warned against the "spirit of party" and foreign influence, which he saw as "one of the most baneful foes of Republican Government."

Washington returned to Mount Vernon following the inauguration of his successor and former vice-president, John Adams, on March 4, 1797; his journey home was marked by popular demonstrations of affection and esteem. At Mount Vernon, which had suffered from neglect during his absence, he resumed the plantation life he loved. He had ceased purchasing slaves in 1772 and "wished from his soul" that Virginia could be persuaded to abolish slavery—"it might prevent much future mischief"—but by this time Washington was too old to attempt another revolution.

Washington came out of retirement one last time, in July 1798, to accept (reluctantly) an appointment as lieutenant-general to command a provisional army of defense in anticipation of war with France. Washington and his Federalist friends were concerned that the

From George Washington's Last Will and Testament

It is my Will and desire that all the Slaves which I hold in my own right, shall receive their freedom. . . . And whereas among those who will receive freedom according to this devise, there may be some, who from old age or bodily infirmities, and others who on account of their infancy, that will be unable to support themselves; it is my Will and desire that all who come under the first and second description shall be comfortably cloathed and fed by my heirs while they live; and that such of the latter description as have no parents living, or if living are unable, or unwilling to provide for them, shall be bound by the Court until they shall arrive at the age of twenty-five years. The Negroes thus bound, are (by their Masters and Mistresses) to be taught to read and write; and to be brought up to some useful occupation, agreeably to the Laws of the Commonwealth of Virginia, providing for the support of Orphan and other poor Children.

Opposite: List of slaves at Mount Vernon (July 1799) by George Washington. By the 1790s, Washington and his wife owned over 300 slaves. Unlike many of his contemporaries, Washington was profoundly disturbed by the institution of slavery and foresaw that it would cause great conflicts in the decades to come. In his will (see above), he granted freedom to all of his slaves, while Martha's remained property of the Custis family after her death.

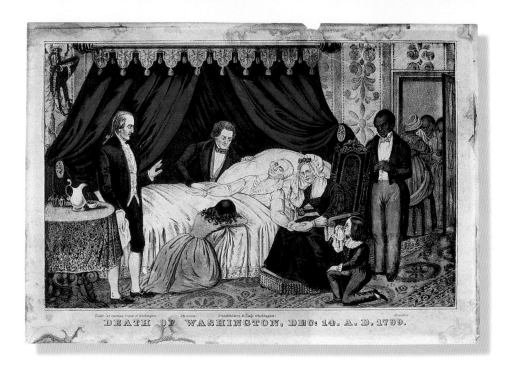

DEATH OF WASHINGTON, DEC: 14. A.D. 1799.

Above: **Death of George Washington, Dec. 14 a.d. 1799 (1846) by James Baillie. Washington braved cold rains and wind as he made the rounds of Mount Vernon on December 12. The next day, he came down with a sore throat but forged ahead with outdoor work near the house. His condition worsened rapidly and he died the next day despite doctors' efforts to save him with such remedies as bleeding and a blister of cantharides on the throat. Just before he died, according to his secretary, Tobias Lear, he felt his own pulse; his countenance changed; "and he expired without a struggle or a sigh."**

French might invade and even overthrow the government with the help of "the French party," by which they meant the Jeffersonian Republicans: "Having struggled for eight or nine years against the invasion of our rights by one power, and to establish an independence of it, I could not remain an unconcerned spectator of the attempt of another power to accomplish the same object though in a different way." The war did not materialize, and in the months that followed Washington devoted himself increasingly to the management of Mount Vernon.

On December 13, 1799, Washington came down with a sudden illness, and he died at Mount Vernon the next day. He was buried in the family vault at Mount Vernon after a simple ceremony.

George Washington will always be remembered as the embodiment of virtue, moderation, and incorruptibility, a second Cincinnatus "called from the plow to lead a great nation."

Washington Eulogized

"A citizen, first in war, first in peace, and first in the hearts of his countrymen."

Henry "Light Horse Harry" Lee, December 26, 1799

"He was, in every sense, a wise, a good, and a great man. Never did nature and fortune combine more perfectly to make a man great, and to place him in the same constellation with whatever worthies have merited from man an everlasting remembrance."

Thomas Jefferson, January 2, 1814

"Washington is the mightiest name of earth—long since mightiest in the cause of civil liberty, still mightiest in moral reformation. In solemn awe we pronounce the name, and in its naked deathless splendor leave it shining on."

Abraham Lincoln, February 22, 1842

Apotheosis of Washington (1802–1810). After his death, the respect and reverence for Washington often lapsed into deification, something which he would have certainly forbidden during his lifetime. Nevertheless, his character and great achievements were exemplary during the turbulent centuries to come, when many Americans rued the fact that they did not have another Washington to guide the nation.

Chronology

1732 February 22 Born at the family home at Popes Creek, Westmoreland County, Virginia

1743 April 12 Washington's father Augustine died at age 49.

1749 July 20 Appointed surveyor of Culpeper County, Virginia

1751 September 1751–March 1752 Sailed to Barbados with half-brother Lawrence Washington

1752 November 6 Appointed major in the Virginia Militia

1754 July 4 Surrendered to French after defeat at Fort Necessity

1755 May 10 Appointed volunteer aide-de-camp to General Edward Braddock
July 9 Braddock was mortally wounded, army defeated at Monongahela River; Washington won praise for his courage in battle.
August 14 Appointed Colonel and Commander of the Virginia regiment

1758 July 24 Elected Burgess for Frederick County, Virginia (re-elected May 18, 1761)
November Fort DuQuesne was abandoned by French; Washington resigned his commission.

1759 January 6 Married Martha (Dandridge) Custis

1761 March 14 Ann Fairfax Washington Lee, widow of Lawrence, died.

1765 July 16 Elected to Virginia House of Burgesses for Fairfax county (re-elected 1768, 1769, 1771, 1774)

1773 May–June Journey to New York City
June 19 Martha (Patsy) Parke Custis died at age 17 during an epileptic seizure.

1774 August Attended first Virginia Provincial Convention in Williamsburg
August 1 Elected to attend First Continental Congress in Philadelphia
September–October First Continental Congress was held in Philadelphia.

1775 May–June Delegate at Second Continental Congress
June 16 Elected General and Commander-in-Chief of the Army of the United States
July 3 Took command of Continental troops at Cambridge, Massachusetts

1776 March 16 Washington's troops drove the British out of Boston after an eight-month seige.
July 4 Signing of the Declaration of Independence
July 9 Declaration was read aloud to each brigade on Washington's recommendation.
August 27–29 Americans were defeated at Battle of Long Island; retreated to Manhattan.
September 19 New York City was burned by patriot arsonists.
October 28 Americans were defeated at White Plains, New York.
December 25 Washington and his troops re-crossed the Delaware River.
December 26 Hessians were defeated at Trenton, New Jersey.

1777 January 3 British were defeated at Battle of Trenton; Washington established winter quarters at Morristown, New Jersey.
September 11 Americans were defeated at the Battle of the Brandywine.
October 4 Americans were defeated at the Battle of Germantown.
October 17 Burgoyne surrendered at Saratoga, New York.

1778 June 18 British evacuated Philadelphia.
June 28 British were defeated at the Battle of Monmouth.

1780 July 11 French fleet and army arrived at Newport, Rhode Island, under the command of Rochambeau.

1781 September 9–12 Stopped at Mount Vernon for the first time since 1775
October 19 British, under command of Cornwallis, surrendered at Yorktown.
November 5 John Parke (Jacky) Custis, Washington's stepson, died at age 28. George and Martha Washington adopted his two youngest children, Nelly and George Washington Custis, and raised them at Mount Vernon.

1783 March 15 Newburgh Address
June 19 Elected president-general of the Society of the Cincinnati
November 2 Bade farewell to his army
December 4 Bade farewell to his officers in Fraunces Tavern in Lower Manhattan
December 23 Resigned his commission to Congress at Annapolis

1784 December Attended Annapolis Conference on
Potomac River navigation

1785 March 23–25 Hosts Mount Vernon Conference
May 17 Elected president of the Potomac Company
October 2 Sculptor Jean-Antoine Houdon visited
Mount Vernon.

1787 May 25 Attended Philadelphia Convention and
was at once elected its president
September 17 Draft of Constitution was signed
at Philadelphia; Federal Convention was adjourned.

1788 January 18 Elected Chancellor of William and
Mary College
June 21 New Hampshire ratified the U.S.
Constitution, the ninth and deciding vote.

1789 February 4 Elected
President of the United
States by unanimous
vote in the Electoral
College
April 30
Inaugurated at
Federal Hall in New
York City
August 25 Washington's mother,
Mary Ball Washington, died at Fredericksburg,
Virginia.
October–November Presidential tour of
New England (except Rhode Island)

1790 September Arrived in Philadelphia, the new
(temporary) capital of the United States

1791 April–June Presidential tour of the southern
United States
December 15 Bill of Rights was ratified

1792 December 5 Unanimously re-elected for a second
term as President of the United States

1793 March 4 Inaugurated for second term
at Pennsylvania State House
(Independence Hall), Philadelphia
April 22 Issued proclamation of
neutrality when France declared
war on Britain
September 18 Laid cornerstone of
Capitol in Federal City (Washington, D.C.)
December 31 Thomas Jefferson
resigned as Secretary of State.

Left: Washington was an active Freemason, and his Masonic ornament decorated the coffin at his funeral.

1794 November Whiskey Rebellion collapsed when
Washington led 12,000 troops into western
Pennsylvania.

1795 January 31 Alexander Hamilton resigned as
Secretary of Treasury.
August 14 Signed Jay's Treaty with Britain

1796 September 19 Farewell Address published in the
Philadelphia *American Daily Advertiser*

1797 March 4 Retired to Mount Vernon after inauguration of his successor and former vice-president,
John Adams

1798 July 4 Appointed lieutenant-general of the New
Army of the United States

1799 December 14 Died at Mount Vernon
December 18 Buried in the family vault at Mount
Vernon

1802 May 22 Martha Washington died at Mount Vernon.

Opposite: Dove of peace weathervane atop Mount Vernon. Left: Argand lamp purchased by Washington.

CREDITS

Front endpaper: *Celebration of Washington's Birthday at Malta on Board U.S.S. Constitution, Commodore Jesse Elliot* (1837) by James G. Evans, Naval Academy Museum, Annapolis.

Page 1, Bust of George Washington (1785) by Jean-Antoine Houdon, courtesy of the Mount Vernon Ladies' Association.

Page 2, Washington family coat of arms, (14th century), photographer Brian Shuel/Collections

Page 3, *George Washington in the Uniform of a British Colonial Colonel* (1772) by Charles Willson Peale, Washington-Custis-Lee Collection, Washington and Lee University, Lexington, Virginia.

Page 4, *Washington and Fairfax at a War Dance* (1857) by John Rogers after John McNevin, courtesy of the Mount Vernon Ladies' Association.

Page 4, Fishing tackle box, Edward Owen photographer, courtesy of the Mount Vernon Ladies' Association.

Page 5, Braddock's sword, Edward Owen photographer, courtesy of the Mount Vernon Ladies' Association.

Page 5, *Washington Crossing the Allegheny River* (c. 1844) by D. Kimberley after Daniel Huntington, courtesy of the Mount Vernon Ladies' Association.

Page 6, Braddock's sash, courtesy of the Mount Vernon Ladies' Association.

Page 6-7, *Washington as a Captain in the French and Indian War* (1849-56) by Junius Brutus Stearns, Virginia Museum of Fine Arts, Richmond. Gift of Edgar William and Bernice Chrysler Garbisch. Photo: Ron Jennings, Virginia Museum of Fine Arts.

Page 8, Painting of Mount Vernon (c. 1792) attributed to Edward Savage, Edward Owen photographer, courtesy of the Mount Vernon Ladies' Association.

Page 8, Martha Parke Custis and John Parke Custis miniatures, Robert Lautman photographer, courtesy of the Mount Vernon Ladies' Association.

Page 9, Plan of Mount Vernon's grounds, Edward Owen photographer, courtesy of the Mount Vernon Ladies' Association.

Page 10, *The Bloody Massacre perpetrated in Boston on March 5th 1770*, printed by Paul Revere, Gilder-Lehrman Collection, on deposit at the Pierpont Morgan Library/Art Resource, New York.

Page 11, Colonial currency, Edward Owen photographer, courtesy of the Mount Vernon Ladies' Association.

Page 12, Flintlock pistol, Edward Owen photographer, courtesy of the Mount Vernon Ladies' Association.

Page 12, Copper nameplate, courtesy of the Mount Vernon Ladies' Association.

Page 13, *The Bostonians Paying the Exise-Man, or Tarring & Feathering* (1774), Gilder-Lehrman Collection, on deposit at the Pierpont Morgan Library/Art Resource, New York.

Page 14, *Burning of New York City*, courtesy of the Mount Vernon Ladies' Association.

Page 15, *Washington Crossing the Delaware* (1853), courtesy of the Mount Vernon Ladies' Association.

Page 16, Miniatures and Bastille key, Edward Owen photographer, courtesy of the Mount Vernon Ladies' Association.

Page 17, *Washington and his Generals at Yorktown* (1781-83) by Charles Willson Peale, Maryland Historical Society, Baltimore.

Page 18, Washington's uniform, Charles Phillips photographer, National Museum of American History.

Page 19, *Washington as a Farmer in Mount Vernon* (1851) by Junius Brutus Stearns (detail), Virginia Museum of Fine Arts. Gift of Edgar William and Bernice Chrysler Garbisch. Photo: Ron Jennings, Virginia Museum of Fine Arts.

Page 20, Bust of George Washington (1785) by Jean-Antoine Houdon, courtesy of the Mount Vernon Ladies' Association.

Page 21, Gold watch, Edward Owen photographer, courtesy of the Mount Vernon Ladies' Association.